WHEN SNIGLETS RULED THE EARTH

RICH HALL

Illustrated by Arnie Ten

Edited by Ann Slichter and Pat Tourk Lee

LARSENTIOUS *(lar sen' tee us')* adj. Consulting *The Far Side* before addressing any other part of the newspaper.

WHEN SNIGLETS RULED THE EARTH

(snig' lit):
any word that doesn't appear in the dictionary, but should

Collier Books • Macmillan Publishing Company • New York
Collier Macmillan Publishers • London

Collier Books
Macmillan Publishing Company
866 Third Avenue, New York, N.Y. 10022
Collier Macmillan Canada, Inc.

Library of Congress Cataloging-in-Publication Data
Hall, Rich, 1954–
    When sniglets ruled the earth: (snig′lit), any word that doesn't
appear in the dictionary, but should/Rich Hall; illustrated by
Arnie Ten; edited by Ann Slichter.
      p.   cm.
    ISBN 0-02-040441-7
    1. Words, New—English—Humor.   2. Vocabulary—Humor.
I. Slichter, Ann. II. Title.
PN6231.W64H344   1988
428.1′0207—dc19   89-652   CIP

10 9 8 7 6 5 4 3 2 1
Designed by Antler & Baldwin, Inc.
PRINTED IN THE UNITED STATES OF AMERICA

To Skylar

Creative Assistant, Margaret Weber

CONTENTS

ABANDABAG
(uh ban' da bag)

n. The suitcase that keeps going around and around the luggage carousel.

ACCIDUE
(ax' ih dew)

n. Small pile of broken glass, chrome, and other debris that remains at the scene several months after an accident.

ACCOMOMAMMADATION
(a kom' oh mam' uh day' shun)

n. The inconspicuous manner in which a woman adjusts a fallen bra strap.

ADHOKUM
(ad' hok um)

n. In commercials, the belief that because the actor is wearing a white lab coat, he must be an expert.

AIREPT
(ayr' ept)

n. Fear of wiping out an entire shelf of souvenirs with one's luggage in an airport gift shop.

AIRSUPIAL
(ayr soop' ee al)

n. On an airplane, the pouch in front of you that holds the airsickness bag and in-flight magazine.

ALPHAFLUB
(al' fuh flub)

n. Any mismatched letter on a movie marquee (i.e., *Fetal Attraction, Running Sacred*).

ALPOLECTIC FIT
(al' po lek' tic fiht')

n. Convulsive state of a dog upon seeing you arrive home in the afternoon.

ALTEATRAZ
(al tee' traz)

n. The small leaves that manage to escape from tea bags.

AQUELLO
(ah kwel' oh)

n. The brilliant yellow that distinguishes all waterproof materials.

ASHTRACTION
(ash trak' shun)

n. The point at which you stop paying attention to what a person is saying and start wondering just how much longer the ash at the end of his cigarette is going to grow before it falls into his lap.

BABO RECLOSO
(ba' bo re kloh' zo)

n. The futile attempt to reseal a Comet can.

BACHSLAPPER
(bahk' slap er)

n. Anyone who applauds the wrong part of a classical concert.

BARCATHROTTLE
(bar' ka throt' uhl)

n. The wooden lever on the side of a recliner that acts like a gearshift.

BARF UNITS
(barf yew' nitz)

n. The number of groups of people you count off in the line ahead of you at an amusement park ride, trying to determine how long before it's your turn.

BATHBURP
(bath' burp)

n. The eerie tendency of a bathtub stop to loudly release itself a few minutes after you've turned off the shower.

THE BELL NUTWORK
(thub bel' nut' work)

n. The system of squirrel transportation provided by telephone lines.

BIMBIO
(bim by' oh)

n. The fictional data on the back side of a *Playboy* centerfold.

BINGOOPS
(bing' go oops)

n. People who prematurely yell "Bingo!" then try to mask the mistake.

BIRDMANTRAS
(bird' man' traz)

n. The point at which repetitive bird chirps begin to sound like human phrases (e.g., "No sleep for you, No sleep for you, No sleep …").

BLIMPLIMENTS
(blimp' lih mentz)

n. The toppings at a low-calorie yogurt parlor that effectively cancel out the whole reason for eating yogurt in the first place.

BOBAROMA
(bob' a roma)

n. Pungent odor that remains in the air after using aerosol hair spray.

BOGUSH
(bo' gush)

v. Obligatorily spouting phrases like "I'll call you soon" at the end of a date because you can't think of anything else to say.

BOOPCHATTER
(boop' chat ur)

n. The series of high-pitched beeps you hear at the beginning and end of prerecorded cassette tapes.

BOXSQUATTERS
(box' skwa terz)

n. Baseball fans who wait until the third or fourth inning and then sneak down to better seats.

BUBBLEWEISER
(bub' bel why' zur)

n. The yellow liquid found in a carpenter's level.

BUNIONETTE
(bun' yun et)

n. Any young professional woman in a business suit and Reeboks.

CAESAR'S TAHOLDERS
(see' zarz tah' hold erz)

n. The plastic cup old ladies hold their quarters in at casinos.

CARJONES
(kar hoh' nez)

n. The incredible bravery one possesses as long as you are inside your car.

CARTERNITY
(kar tur' nih tee)

n. The law that says characters in a comic strip will remain the same age forever.

22 CARTHRITIS
(karth wry' tis)

n. The pathetic struggle of an old power window to make that last inch.

CATPLAST
(kat' plast)

n. The built-in element that allows a cat to occasionally stretch himself to astounding lengths.

CATTARACT
(kat' ar act)

n. Any fat Garfield cat attached to a car window that partially obstructs a driver's vision.

CENTSTRESS
(sent' stres)

n. Anxiety felt during the mad scramble for loose change when the cashier says, "Do you have a penny?"

CHINDEPENDENTS
(chin' de pen' dents)

n. The few hairs that always remain after shaving that you don't notice until several hours later.

CHIPLINGER
(chip' ling er)

n. The bits of raw vegetables and broken snacks that blend into a dip during a large party.

CINEPEDS
(sin' ih pedz)

n. The feet that mysteriously appear over your shoulders when you're trying to watch a movie.

CINETWERP
(sin' ih twerp)

n. Any cinema employee who has the nerve to ask you for exact change because the tickets have been jacked up to $7.50.

CLOBBERISM
(klahb' ur iz' um)

n. Strange array of verbs used by sportscasters to explain the outcome of a game (e.g., "Lakers *drowned* the Nets, Bears *clawed* the Vikings").

COAXIOMS
(ko ax' ee umz)

n. When shopping for stereo equipment, the incoherent techno-phrases salesmen use (e.g., "dynamic audio range," "frequency modulation") that you nod along with and pretend to understand.

COMIMORPHISM
(ko mim' orf ih' zem)

n. Cutting out cartoons and assigning real-life names to the characters.

COMMON DENUMBINATOR
(kaw' mun dih num' ih nay' tor)

n. The point in a first date where you realize you have nothing in common with the person you're with, and you begin plotting how to get out of it.

COMPIZZABLE
(kom peez' a bul)

adj. The capacity of a group to actually agree upon toppings for a pizza ("Okay, no pepperoni, but we've got to have mushrooms").

CONISMA
(kohn ih' zmuh)

n. The tendency of American drivers to obey and follow traffic cones no matter where they lead.

CONSPICUSLAT
(kon' spic u' slat)

n. A strip in a set of venetian blinds that has a different slant than the others.

CONTINENTATER
(kon' tih nent ay' tor)

n. The guy at the map making company who decides what color each state should be.

CREDIDIOTS
(kred id' ee utz')

n. People who linger during the credits on a movie, as if they are going to recognize someone ("Look, honey, Ed Kremetski was the key grip").

CRITIGASM
(krit' ih gaz' um)

n. Any gushing critical blurb given to a movie that guarantees the reviewer's name will appear larger than anyone else's in the movie ad.

CUMULASTICS
(kewm' uhl as' tiks)

n. The collection of rubber bands on a person's doorknob.

DECIBILATION
(des' ih bul' ay shun')

n. Shock of having your personal stereo headphones yanked out of your ears by normally passive objects (such as elbows, coattails, watchband, etc.).

DENTOCRAM
(den toe kram')

n. The foolish attempt to achieve a year's worth of brushing and flossing an hour before your dentist appointment.

DIANKULAR
(dy ank' uhl ar)

adj. "Crossover" style of lacing athletic shoes.

DIESELDIAPER
(dee' zul dy' pur)

n. The red flag hanging off the back of a lumber truck.

DIETRIBE
(dy' uh tribe)

n. All the "daily specials" you allow a waiter to reel off even though you know what you want.

DISCOMBEBOPULATE
(dis' kom bee' bop u' layt)

v. To turn down the car radio when you're looking for a street, as if somehow this will help you locate it easier.

DISPATCH TRACK
(dis' pach trak')

n. The squiggly lines next to a postmark on a letter that resemble tire tread marks.

DOG GASKETS
(dog gas' ketz)

n. The black stuff that collects around an elderly dog's mouth.

DRYPHOON
(dry foon')

n. The hot blast of air you always feel when you pass a laundromat.

EARTHCAKE EPICENTER
(urth' kayk ep' ih sen' tur)

n. The buttery, syrup-laden heart of a stack of pancakes . . . the part you save until last.

ENAMELISMS
(ee nam' ulh iz' umz)

n. Overly embellished names given to interior paints to distinguish them from others, such as Mediterranean Sunset and Autumn Harvest.

ENVELOPTIC
(en vel op' tik)

n. Anyone who peers through the box opening at the post office to see if the employees inside are "screwing off."

ETCHACHACHA
(etch' ah cha' cha)

v. The jerky movements your arms and hips make when erasing an Etch-A-Sketch.

FATLAS
(fat' las)

n. The weekly food section crammed full of recipes, coupons, and full-color dessert photos that make a newspaper noticeably heavier.

FLOURESE
(flor' eez)

n. The language you speak while your teeth are being cleaned, discernible only by your dentist.

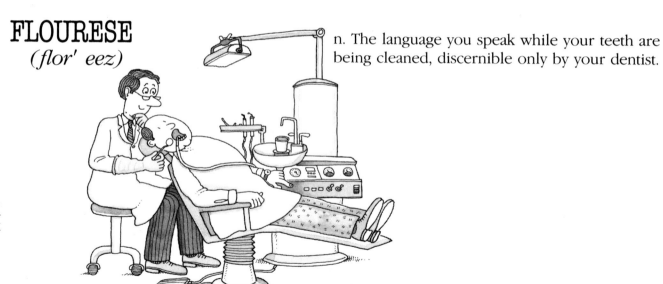

FOOFUMBLERS
(foo' fum blurz)

n. Chopstick nonparticipants at Chinese restaurants.

FRIGIDALIEN
(frij' id ay' lee un)

n. Any nonfood object (batteries, camera film, etc.) kept in the refrigerator to prolong its freshness.

FURPLAY
(fur' play)

n. Semi-illicit feeling you get when a cat rubs against your leg.

GASTIDIOUS
(gas tid' ee us)

GAZOONTING
(ga zoon' ting)

adj. Deft manner in which one removes a gas cap so as not to get any fuel on one's hands.

v. Using one's nose to fold back the pages of a newspaper.

GAZUREALISM
(gaz' ur real izm)

n. While at the museum, having the feeling that the eyes on a portrait are staring directly at you.

GEEZLEFLEW
(geez uhl' floo)

n. Any obtuse object attached to a service station restroom key to prevent you from stealing it.

GIXLET
(gicks' let)

n. A gift you bought for a forgotten relative at 10:57 P.M. on Christmas Eve with five dollars in your budget.

GLACIA PHOBIA
(glay' sha foh bee' ah)

n. A fear occurring in the winter that the snowball a kid holds has your name on it.

GOLFLUORESCENCE
(gol' flor es' ens)

n. On a golf course, the incredibly phosphorescent clothing style adopted by men who otherwise dress rationally.

GOOPWASTE
(goop' wayst)

n. Smearing excess hand lotion on parts of your body that don't need it.

GREAT WALL OF CHINOS
(grayt wahl uf chee' nohs)

v. Shoving a hand into your jeans and discovering the pocket is jammed up.

GRIDLOTT
(grid' lot)

n. Congestion created at checkout lines in convenience or liquor stores by some jerk cashing in a one-dollar lottery ticket.

GUMIPLAST
(gum' ee plast)

n. Two gummy bears fused together.

GUPTOPIA
(gup' toh pee yuh)

n. The phony decor in an aquarium designed to fool fish into thinking they're in an underwater paradise.

HANCROCK
(han' crawk)

n. A signature usually found on diplomas and corporate checks that has been stamped there as opposed to handwritten.

HEADWEASELS
(hed' wee' zulz)

n. Snooty, pompous, overbearing maître d's who address you in the third person: "How many are we tonight?"

HIESTENATION
(hyst' en ay' shun)

n. The sudden inviting notion you get when seeing an open bank vault that maybe, just maybe, you could get away with it.

HOPNO
(hohp' no)

n. Emergency repair of a hem with staples (which you hope no one notices).

HOROSCOPIA
(hor' o sco' pee uh)

n. The lingo or advice in a horoscope that can be applied to any person in any circumstance.

IDPRESSION
(id pre' shun)

n. Attempt to stifle laughter upon viewing someone's driver's license.

INCOMEPOOP
(in' kum poop)

n. The smell on storekeepers' fingers from handling money all day.

INCONSMUTULOUS
(in' kon smut' u lus')

adj. Buying extraneous magazines to help camouflage *Playboy* or *Penthouse*.

INCUISINATORS
(in kwiz ih' nay torz')

n. People at adjoining restaurant tables who seem more interested in your food than their own.

INDIGESTURES
(in dih jest' jurz)

n. The hollow gestures and halfhearted protestations you feel required to make when someone else is picking up the check.

INKFLAMATION
(ink' fla may' shun)

n. The point at which the ink pen you're chewing on begins to taste like ink, causing you to suspect that it's all over your mouth.

INTUNATIVE
(in toon' a tiv')

adj. Mentally hearing a song begin on an album seconds before it actually plays.

INTUXICATION
(in tux' ih kay' shun)

n. Confusion as to whether the ribbed openings on a cummerbund are supposed to face up or down.

JACK O'LOBOTOMY
(jak o' loh bot' o mee)

v. Removing pulp and seeds from a pumpkin.

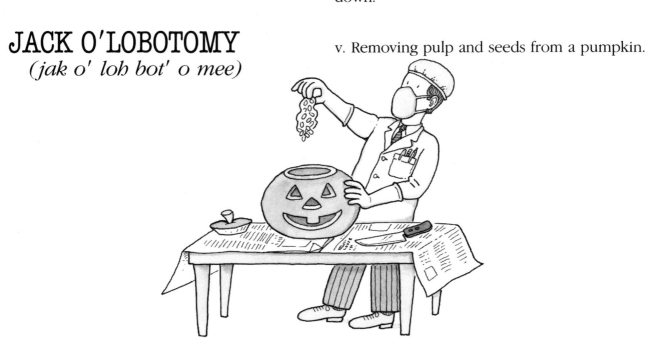

JETSCHPIEL
(jet' shpeel)

n. The animated "safety speech" given by flight attendants that most frequent flyers ignore.

KRASHTONITE
(krash' ton ite)

n. The indestructible material the "black box" is made of—and how come the rest of the plane isn't made of this?

KROGERPHOBIA
(kroh' gur fob' ee uh)

n. The fear that everyone suspects you of shoplifting when you try to leave a store without buying anything.

LARSENTIOUS
(lar sen' tee us')

adj. Consulting *The Far Side* before addressing any other part of the newspaper.

LAVORTEX
(lav' or tex)

n. Megasuction force of airplane toilets that banishes the slightest piece of toilet paper deep into the bowels of the plane's interior.

LEBBETTS
(leb' betz)

n. The mangled pieces of bread that people pass over thinking the stuff in the middle is "fresher."

LINGERUISTICS
(ling' er wis' tiks)

n. The phenomenon of staring at a word so long it begins to look misspelled.

LIPPLE
(lih' pul)

n. All the stuff that collects around the outside of a Chapstick lid after it's been in your pocket.

LOBSTERINE
(lahb' ster een)

n. The green stuff that oozes from the center of the lobster.

LOOBLAZE
(loo' blayz)

n. The blinding glare you feel when you turn on the lights at 3 A.M. to go to the bathroom.

LOSERLITTER
(loo' zur lih' tur)

n. Accumulation of losing tickets on a racetrack floor.

LOUISPRIMADONNA
(loo' ee pree' ma don' uh)

n. The snobbish manner in which a woman always carries a Louis Vuitton purse.

MALLCONTENTS
(mawl' kon' tentz)

n. The collection of bored, ticked-off husbands you always see sitting on benches in the middle of a shopping mall.

MARKAHOLIC WARD
(mark' uh hol' ik ward')

n. The place in your desk where you send dried-out felt tip pens to recover.

MATRIPHOBIA
(mat' rih fo' bee uh')

n. Noticeable distance that single men keep from the woman who just caught the bouquet at a wedding.

MAYBELO
(may' bel oh)

n. The space a woman makes with her mouth when applying makeup.

MELBLANGUAGE
(mel blan' gwij)

n. The conversation baby boomers engage in when discussing their favorite cartoon.

MEOUCH
(mee' owch)

n. The part of a cat's neck that you're allowed to grab and lift (although the cat never appears to be convinced of this).

MERLIN'S SUDS
(mur' linz sudz)

n. While washing dishes, what makes a wet glass or dish mysteriously travel across a counter top.

MESOGROOVIC
(mez' oh groov' ik)

adj. Type of people who enter onto a dance floor already in motion.

MIASMA VICE
(my' az muh vys)

n. Background smoke used in film scenes to create a mood of impending danger.

MICHEMANCY
(mish' uh man' see)

n. Idle prediction of what part of the world James Michener will epicly attack next.

MILD CORNARY
(mild corn' ayr ee)

n. Any reaction to the price of movie popcorn.

MIRRORABILIA
(mih rawr' uh beel' ee uh)

n. The useless junk (air fresheners, miniature running shoes, mortar board tassels) hanging from the rearview mirror.

MITSTIGATE
(mitz' tih gayt)

v. Pounding your baseball mitt right before a pitch as if this will somehow lure the ball toward you.

MODADS or HODADS
(mo' dadz or ho' dadz)

n. All the free stuff (shampoo, moisturizer, sewing kits) one feels compelled to take when checking out of a motel/hotel (under the assumption the next place you stay will be a real dump).

MOFFLIES
(maw' flyz)

n. Geezers who materialize at construction sites and feel compelled to point out that whatever it is you're doing . . . you're doing it wrong.

MONOPYOLOED
(mon' op yoh' lohd)

n. Person controlling the largest empire on a Monopoly game.

MOUTHLETIC
(mowth' let ik)

adj. Having the useless talent acquired in bars of being able to twist a cherry stem into a knot with one's tongue.

MOWERHAWK
(moh' er hawk')

n. The strip of grass that remains here and there after mowing a lawn.

MUFFINLUST
(muh' fin lust)

n. The slightly illicit feeling one experiences when undressing a cupcake.

NABULANCE
(nab' yoo lants)

n. As viewed by the cop who just pulled you over, the *slow,* nonchalant appearance of a hand growing out of your neck and groping for the unbuckled seat belt above you.

NADCATCHER
(nad cach' ur)

n. The bar on a man's bicycle that painfully reminds him he's a man.

NEBULAND
(neb' bu land)

n. Any place where the "void where prohibited" clause on a game card appears.

OLINGO
(oh ling' oh)

v. Adding an *o* to the end of a word to make it more colorful, emphatic, etc. (e.g., "Nutso").

OPUKUM
(oh pewk' um)

n. That horrible-looking liquid the scooper sits in at the ice cream parlor.

ORCHIDAIR
(or kid' ayr)

n. The giant see-through refrigerator at the florist where they keep expensive flowers.

OUIJAUL BOARD
(wee' hawl bord)

n. The collection of business and service cards ("We Haul Anything") you see posted on the wall in some laundromats.

PARSLEYCUTION
(par' slee cu' shun)

n. The destruction of garnish on your plate out of fear it will be recycled.

PATLAPSE
(pat' laps)

n. The amount of True Value ad copy Pat Summerall reads before he *finally* says: "Hi, I'm Pat Summerall."

PERPHEW
(pur' few)

n. The overpowering aroma of a thousand colognes that assault you when you enter a department store.

PERPIDANKULAR
(per' pihd dank' uhl ar)

adj. "Parallel" style of lacing athletic shoes.

PETAPHOR
(pet uh' for)

n. Any descriptive phrase that includes an animal ("sick as a dog," "crazy like a fox," etc.).

PHOTARD
(fo' tard)

n. Any oversized head in a high school yearbook, the result of not being present on photo day.

PITJUDICE
(pit' ju dis)

n. The assumption that any breed of dog you can't recognize is a killer pit bull.

PLADONIUM
(play' don ee' um)

n. The unique smell of new Play-doh that almost makes you want to eat it.

PLASTIPAPERPLEXION
(plas' tih pay' pur plec' shun)

n. Confrontation with a supermarket bag boy.

PRESSTENTIVE
(pres ten' tiv)

n. The one newspaper that gets passed around an entire coffee shop.

PUKETORIALS
(pewk' tor ee alz)

n. The lush photographs and thoughtful "serving suggestions" offered by frozen dinner manufacturers in an attempt to make the food inside more palatable.

PUZZ
(puz)

n. The stuff that collects at the bottom of a jigsaw puzzle box.

Q-SPICIOUS
(ku' spih' shus)

adj. Examining a cotton swab immediately after use to make sure part of your brain isn't attached to it.

QUANTATO
(qwan tay' toe)

n. Any french fry so overloaded with ketchup it has to be suspended above and then lowered into one's mouth.

RAGPOLE
(rag' pole)

n. In libraries, the bamboo that is attached to newspapers.

RAYCOON
(ray' koon)

n. Any person who falls asleep sunbathing with shades on and achieves a "masked" look.

RAZOR BAKUS
(raz' or bak' us)

v. Tightening your jaw like Mr. Howell on "Gilligan's Island" in order to get a closer shave.

RE
(ar' ee)

n. The white filling in an Oreo cookie.

REEDGES
(ree' jes)

n. The distinctive ridges on a Reese's cup.

RETRACTABEEPING
(ree trak' ta bee' ping)

v. Explaining to another driver via a series of frantic hand gestures that you honked by accident.

RINFRAKS
(rin' frax)

n. The small pile of broken cones at an ice cream shop.

ROOMSKILLETS
(room' skihl' etz)

n. Those giant eight-ounce keys some hotels give you.

SAFEWAIF
(sayf' wayf)

n. That abandoned half-filled shopping cart you see in a supermarket aisle apparently left by someone who was only "pretending" to be shopping.

SCRATCHTASY
(skrach' ta see)

n. State of euphoria reached when scratching any itch.

SENTIMUCK
(sent' ih muk)

n. The gloopy feeling you get when you see a newly married couple stuffing cake in each other's face.

$\dfrac{75}{\text{sen}}$

SHOECIDE
(shu' syd)

n. One abandoned shoe in the road.

SHRIMPEDIMENT
(shrim ped' ih ment')

n. The point on a shrimp's tail that you cannot eat past.

SHUSS SHOCK
(shus' shok)

n. The sensation of still wearing skis on your feet several hours after you've removed them.

SKYLIE
(sky' ly)

n. The phony backdrop of a city skyline you see on "David Letterman" and the "Tonight Show."

SLOOPHAPPY
(sloop' hap' ee)

adj. Condition of people on boats who feel compelled to wave at every landlocked person they pass.

SS PALMOIL

SLURPEESLOPPY
(slur' pee slah' pee)

adj. Style of attire worn to a convenience store after 11 P.M.

SNIPOCRIT
(snih' po krit)

n. One who silently scrutinizes the hairdresser's hair before deciding whether to turn his own head over to this person.

SNOOTIQUETTE
(snoo' tih keht)

n. Upgrading one's table manners in direct proportion to the prices on the menu.

SPEEB
(speeb)

n. The beeping noises made by construction or service vehicles when they are backing up.

SPLATFORM
(splat' form)

n. The step on a ladder boldly marked THIS IS NOT A STEP.

SPRUCE SPRIGSTEENS
(sproos sprig' steenz)

n. Those pine-scented car fresheners (see MIRRORABILIA) you see from some rearview mirrors.

SQUEALLICIT
(skwee' lih sit)

v. Missing a freeway exit by a few feet and backing up, rather than continuing to the next stop.

STATIGROOVIC
(stat ih' groov' ik)

adj. Type of people who wait until they're *on* the dance floor to begin dancing.

STEREOIDS
(stayr' ee oydz)

n. Mysterious packet included in some hi-fi products to keep them fresh.

STRATEGIC TART LIMITATION
(stra tee' jik tart lim' ih tay' shun)

n. The compromise reached by two people who know they shouldn't have dessert but are secretly dying for it.

SUITICIDE NOTES
(soot' ih syd' notes)

n. Apologetic "We tried but . . ." note you find on pieces of dry cleaning you didn't even know were stained to begin with (leading you to believe the dry cleaner probably created the stain).

SWANTHRACITE
(swan' thra syt)

n. The part of a TV dinner that remains semifrozen even after microwaving.

SWIMSWANKY
(swim' swank' ee)

adj. The superhuman ability of the watersliding victims on an airline safety card to stay dry and perfectly groomed.

TANNENBUM
(tah' nen buhm)

n. The least attractive side of a Christmas tree—the undecorated side that faces the wall.

TELESUCKIE
(tele suh' kee)

v. The act of holding a phone receiver to your chest as you dial.

TESTPIRATE
(test' pur ayt)

v. To emit a big gush of air from one's lungs after turning in an exam.

THRIFT SHOCK
(thrihft' shok)

n. Spotting previously owned items at a Salvation Army.

TICKIDIOT
(tik' id ee' ut)

n. What you feel like when you've just "thanked" a police officer for a speeding ticket.

TONKATIVE
(tonk' a tiv)

adj. When a kid makes up his own soundtrack to accompany the miniature cars he's playing with on the floor.

TUPPERZOID
(tup' er zoid)

n. The mysterious monster who enters the dishwasher during the cycle and melts spatula handles and plastic bowls.

TYLEXIC
(ty lex' ik)

n. Stranglehold position one is forced to adopt when trying to help a kid knot a necktie.

UNCLE BEN'S RABIES
(unk' l benz ray' beez)

n. Cascade created when one adds rice to boiling water.

UNDERWONDER
(un' dur won' dur)

n. That "knowing" feeling you get when carrying an armload of laundry that causes you to turn and look behind and see a trail of dropped underwear.

VEGAS VASELINE
(vay' gas vaz' eh leen)

n. The invisible product that seasoned tippers use to slip a gratuity into a maître d's palm without showing any "green" whatsoever.

VIDEO K. CORRAL
(vid' ee oh kay' kor' al)

n. The gunslinger feeling you get when you're armed with a VCR remote control in one hand and a TV channel control in the other.

VOLTAGRAM
(vult' a gram)

n. The miniature maps inside tape players that show how the batteries should be arranged.

WAISTENATE
(way' sten ayt)

v. Silent calculation of the human tonnage in an elevator to determine if it has exceeded its weight limit.

WIMBLEDOWN
(wim bul' down)

n. The fuzz on tennis balls.

WINDNESTY
(wind' nest ee)

n. The belief that if the parking ticket lodged between your wiper and your windshield blows away, you don't have to pay for it.

WIPERCUSSION
(why' pur kuh' shun)

n. Phenomenon of one's windshield wipers keeping perfect time with the song on the radio.

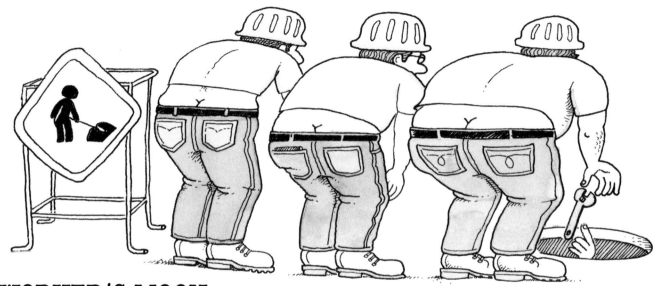

WORKER'S MOON
(wur' kerz mewn')

n. The true international symbol of "men at work."

WUJECTIVE
(woo' jec tiv)

n. Any word consisting of a prefix and a nonexisting baseword (e.g., nonplussed and redundant).

YABBADYNAMICS
(yab' uh dy nam' iks)

n. Propulsive force that enables Fred Flintstone to power a stone automobile with just his feet.

YACHTCHOTSKIS
(yaht chaht' skeez)

n. Ornamental naval etchings you always see carved on the buttons of a man's blazer.

YARDYUTZ
(yar' dee yutz)

n. Home owners who build a circular driveway in front of a two-bedroom house, trying to impress the neighbors.

OFFICIAL SNIGLETS ENTRY BLANK

Dear Rich:

    Here's my sniglet, which is every bit as clever as any in this dictionary:

_____

_____

_____

_____

_____

Sincerely,

(name) _____

(street address) _____

(city, state, zip code) _____

SNIGLETS
P.O. Box 2350
Hollywood, CA 90078